D0183418

Penguins

Patricia Kendell

HODDER
Wayland

An imprint of Hodder Children's Books

Alligators Chimpanzees Dolphins Elephants
Giraffes Gorillas Grizzly Bears Hippos
Leopards Lions Orangutans Pandas Penguins
Polar Bears Rhinos Sea Otters Sharks Tigers

 © 2003 White-Thomson Publishing Ltd

Produced for Hodder Wayland by White-Thomson Publishing Ltd

Editor: Kay Barnham
Designer: Tim Mayer
Consultant: Keith Reid – marine biologist at the British Antarctic
Survey in Cambridge
Language Consultant: Norah Granger – Senior Lecturer in Primary
  Education at the University of Brighton
Picture research: Shelley Noronha – Glass Onion Pictures

Published in Great Britain in 2003 by Hodder Wayland,
an imprint of Hodder Children's Books.
Reprinted in 2004

Photograph acknowledgements:
Bruce Coleman 9, 22 & 32, 28 (Johnny Johnson), 15, 27
(Hans Reinhard); FLPA 25 (Peggy Heard), 24 (David Hosking),
10 (E & D Hosking), 1 & 20, 8, 12, 13, 17, 19, 26 (Minden
Pictures); NHPA 16 (A N T), 18 (Gerard Lacz), 5 (Dr Eckart
Pott), 14 (Kevin Schafer); OSF 7 (Doug Allen), 21 (Tim Jackson),
11 (Colin Monteath), 6 (Konrad Wothe); SPL 4 (Tim Davis),
23 (Gregory Dimijian).

British Library Cataloguing in Publication Data
Kendell, Patricia
  Penguins. – (In the wild)
  1. Penguins – Juvenile literature
  I. Title II. Barnham, Kay
  598.4'7

ISBN: 0 7502 4224 8

Printed and bound in China

Hodder Children's Books
A division of Hodder Headline Limited
338 Euston Road, London NW1 3BH

Produced in association with WWF-UK.
WWF-UK registered charity number 1081247.
A company limited by guarantee number 4016725.
Panda device © 1986 WWF ® WWF registered trademark owner.

Contents

Where penguins live

Penguins are birds that live in and around the sea in the southern half of the world. Many live in Antarctica, where it is very cold.

Some penguins live in warmer places, such
as the Galapagos Islands, near South America.

Penguin eggs

Most penguins lay two eggs in a nest
made of small pebbles.

Emperor penguins lay only one egg.
They rest the egg on their feet and cover
it with a fold of skin to keep it warm.

Looking after the chicks

When the penguin chick hatches from the egg, it is covered in fluffy **down**. Its parents take turns to feed the chick and keep it warm.

When it is old enough, the chick **huddles**
together with other chicks, while both
parents go to find food.

9

Growing up

As they get older, penguin chicks begin to **moult**, losing their downy feathers.

Once they have their adult **waterproof** feathers, they can swim and find food for themselves.

Keeping in touch

Penguins gather together in large groups
called rookeries. They are safer here.

This parent is looking for its chick. Penguins find their chicks by calling them with a special sound that only their chick will recognise.

Getting about

Penguins cannot fly, but they swim very well,
using their wings like flippers.

When they come on land, penguins waddle or hop. Some penguins in Antarctica **toboggan** on their stomachs.

Finding food

Penguins dive deep into the sea to find food. A dive can take over 15 minutes and be deeper than 100 metres.

They look for small shrimp-like creatures
called krill. They also eat small fish and **squid**.

17

Eating and drinking

Penguins can catch fish with their beaks.
These penguins are chasing the same fish!

Penguins drink sea water and get some
of the liquid they need from snow.

Keeping warm ... keeping cool

Penguins in Antarctica have many small, closely packed feathers and a layer of fat to keep them warm.

Penguins that live on hot beaches in South Africa have less fat. They cool off by opening their beaks and panting like dogs.

Keeping safe

Adult penguins watch out for sharks, killer whales and leopard seals. These animals like to eat penguins.

Penguins can swim very fast. This penguin
is jumping out of the water to escape from
a hungry enemy.

Threats ...

Some penguins are leaving the beaches where they nest because people come there. This means fewer eggs are laid.

24

People are taking too many fish out of the sea, leaving less food for the penguins and other sea creatures.

...and dangers

If oil gets into the sea, it can damage a penguin's feathers. This makes it difficult for the penguin to swim and find food.

The Earth is getting warmer. This may mean that these penguin chicks' parents will have to travel further to find food. If the chicks have to wait, they could starve.

Helping penguins to survive

People must work together to stop **oil spills** happening, and make sure there is enough for the penguins to eat.

We must protect the places where penguins live and learn more about what penguins need to survive.

Further information

Find out more about how we can help penguins in the future.

ORGANIZATIONS TO CONTACT

WWF-UK
Panda House, Weyside Park,
Godalming, Surrey GU7 1XR
Tel: 01483 426444
http://www.wwf.org.uk

British Antarctic Survey
High Cross, Madingley Road,
Cambridge CB3 0ET
Tel: 01223 361188
http://www.antarctica.ac.uk/

Monterey Bay Aquarium
886 Cannery Row
Monterey
CA 93940
USA
Tel: 001 831 648 4800
http://www.mbayaq.org

BOOKS

Penguins: Animals of the Ocean: Judith
Hodge-Walker, Barrons Juveniles 1999.
Penguins – First Discovery Book: Rene
Mettler, Cartwheel Books/Scholastic 1996.

Glossary

WEBSITES

Most young children will need adult help when visiting websites. Those listed have child-friendly pages to bookmark.

http://projects.edtech.sandi.net/encanto/penguins
This site invites children to read about five different types of penguin. They are directed to information in order to answer questions about them.

http://www.mbayaq.org/efc/efc_fo/fo_peng_exhibit.asp
This site has information and a video sequence of penguins.

down – the first soft, fluffy feathers of a baby bird.

huddles – crowds together in a group.

moult – to lose first feathers.

oil spills – when oil leaks into the sea, usually from a ship.

squid – a sea animal with long tentacles.

toboggan – to slide over snow or ice.

waterproof – something that keeps water out.

Index